STEPHEN CRANE AT BREDE

An Anglo-American Literary Circle of the 1890's

Gordon Milne

UNIVERSITY
PRESS OF
AMERICA

To Ann and Rosemary

Acknowledgements

I wish to express my appreciation to the Librarians of the University of Illinois Library, the University of Virginia Library and the Library of Congress for having allowed me to examine the H.G. Wells Collection in the Rare Book Room of the University of Illinois Library, the Stephen Crane Collection in the Clifton Waller Barrett Library at the University of Virginia, and the Harold Frederic Papers in the Manuscript Division of the Library of Congress.

Fortuitously clustered together in the south-
eastern corner of England for a brief period at
the very end of the nineteenth century were a
group of writers, British and American. Drawn
somewhat by chance into one another's vicinity in
the early years of the 1890s, they succeeded in
establishing, in their Surrey-Sussex locale, a
distinctly heady literary atmosphere. The linking
figure was Stephen Crane, that "celebrity, even
among other celebrated Americans,"[1] to whose Brede
Place home the others often flocked for visits.
The famous Brede house parties staged by Cora and
Stephen Crane--even if avoided by some members of
the clan as too lively[2]--may serve to symbolize
the pleasant personal associations existing among
them.

In addition to friendship, the group shared,
of course, a dedication to their "trade." Not only
did they respect each other's literary endeavors,
but also they, in some cases, propounded comparable
views of the writer's craft, even composing works
of parallel nature, indeed, even indulging in collaborative efforts. Whether they really influenced
one another's productions is a debatable question,
as is also the degree to which cultural differences
between "Anglo" and "American" set them apart, but
one can surely speculate, both with profit and en-
joyment, about the questions.

The circle included Henry James, Joseph
Conrad, Ford Madox Ford, H.G. Wells, Harold
Frederic, and Crane, with, on the periphery,
figures like Robert Barr, W.H. Hudson, John
Galsworthy, Arnold Bennett, and Edward Garnett.

One notes the English-American mix, and, perhaps more important, the fact that all these men were concerned with technique and the evaluation of prose fiction--even Wells, even Barr--and seriously concerned as well with the problem of man's engagement with "reality." Did they at the same time, one asks again, have any marked effect on each other's work, or was theirs simply a happy and momentary juncture? His fierce insistence on his journalistic role and his mean debunking of James notwithstanding, did not even H.G. Wells feel the impact of this society of litterateurs? Tricky questions to answer with conviction, but the probing for answers may reveal interesting aspects of aesthetic credos, may, more specifically, show something about the development of the twentieth century novel through a transatlantic cooperation.3

* * * * *

Certainly one of the lesser known and less accomplished of the circle was Harold Frederick-- one, too, whose association with the group was cut short by a rather untimely death. As a colorful personality and as a dedicated writer, though, he figured prominently in the London literary life at the century's end. More often than the others in the circle he frequented the literary clubs, enjoying many hours of story-swapping and an exchange of ideas on matters of craft. He probably testified more strongly to the strength of the native American tradition than did James and Crane, too, in that he firmly retained his emotional roots in his own country.4

Frederic moved easily from upper New York State into the intellectual circles of London when, as correspondent for the New York Times, he switched his residence from America to England in the 1880s. Meeting "everybody," from Frank Harris to Sir Charles Dilke, he registered strongly, and in most cases, pleasantly (not with Conrad, who called him a 'gross man who lived grossly and died abominably').[5] Not that he reciprocated everyone's interest and/or affection. Henry James, for one, did not appeal to the flamboyant and earthy Frederic. That "effeminate old donkey who lives with a herd of other donkeys around him and insists on being treated as if he were the Pope . . . has licked dust," said Frederic scornfully, "from the floor of every third rate hostess in England."[6] The outgoing and bumptious Frederic was obviously put off by the prissiness of James, as also by his penchant for attaching himself to the British aristocracy.[7]

Frederic does throw a fair amount of light on the at times uneasy Anglo-American cultural relationship. On the one hand, he resoundingly stressed his American antecedents, telling, in the manner of Joaquin Miller, tall tales to the London clubmen about milking cows on cold winter dawns in Utica,[8] and at the same time stripping some of the glamor from the British aristocracy in books like Gloria Mundi and The Market-Place. On the other hand, he so obviously enjoyed his association with men such as Shaw and Justin McCarthy and profited from his intercourse with them. If his attitude toward English manners and traits remained rather ambivalent, the same might be said of Crane, perhaps even of James.

The question of a circle-inspired influence experienced by Frederic remains inconclusive as well. The group entertained opinions about his work, and, in the case of Crane, the opinions were distinctly favorable. "There was Frederic doing his locality, his Mohawk Valley, with the strong trained hand of a great craftsman," he said. "He is a prodigious laborer. Knowing the man and his methods, one can conceive him doing anything, unless it be writing a poor book."[9] The others offered less enthusiastic comments about his production.

Clearly, Frederic and Crane were most akin, both personally[10] and professionally, sharing, perhaps intuitively, views about the realistic

3

technique, the use of native material, a similarity
of values. If, unlike the Conrad-Ford conjunction,
they added little specifically to each other's art,
yet they shared many interests. Some would say
that James shared them as well:

> . . . like James, whom he cordially
> despised but from whom he appears to
> have learned a good deal, Frederic was
> preoccupied with problems that involve
> moral choices among cogent alternatives.
> Like James he was preoccupied in depth
> with the contemporary problem of the
> self-fulfillment of women and with the
> type of the new woman, toward whom he
> felt some ambivalence.[11]

But it is an "iffy" matter, chance parallels
existing more clearly than specific influences.

Frederic, one has to conclude, remained on
the fringes of the circle. Though his country
home at Kenley placed him in proximity with Conrad
at Ivy Wales Cottage, Wells at Spade House, Barr
at Woldingham, and Crane at Oxted and Brede, even
within range of James at Lamb House, he saw these
"neighbors," save for Crane, rarely. Though they
read his works (e.g., Cora Crane sent a copy of
The Market-Place to James),[12] they tended to dis-
miss him as a clever journalist without sufficient
patience to develop his craft, and certainly they
failed--with the possible exception of Crane[13]--
to be directly affected by his writing. Notwithstanding Gertrude Atherton's claim that "no American writer was ever more appreciated in England,"[14]
one feels sure that Frederic was much more admired
by his friend Grover Cleveland than by the James-
Wells coterie.

* * * * *

About the reputation and the craftsmanship of
Henry James, a slightly more celebrated member of

the group than Frederic, surely little if anything
need be said. It has been said. Even the complex
matter of Anglo-American literary relationship as
affected by James has been dealt with many times,
though problems in this area remain, e.g., does
the "world of letters" altogether transcend nation-
al boundaries as James would probably have it?
was James himself "American" or "Anglo" or "Anglo-
American"? The questions--and basic they are--
still receive a plethora of answers.

The question of James's association with the
group--this, at least, is easily resolved. His
frequent visits to the Cranes at Brede Place are a
matter of record, with photographs as proof positive. One wonders, as he looks at a snapshot of
James posing with Cora Crane, whether the former
knew of his hostess's life before her arrival in
England. Though showing a certain coolness toward
her in the years after Crane's death, he was cor-
diality itself during the Cranes' Brede days. He
was concern, too, sending, at the time of Crane's
last illness, a check for fifty pounds to Cora--
"I've money, moreover I care."[15]

Meetings between James and Ford Madox Ford
occurred almost as often as those with Crane, at
least when Ford was living near Rye at Winchelsea.
The latter indeed laid claim to "a very consider-
able degree of intimacy"[16] with James, though the
friendship suffered in subsequent years after Ford
had established his irregular liaison with Violet
Hunt. The socially conventional James did not
readily sanction the extra-marital activities of
such as Ford and Frederic.

James often encountered Conrad as well, either
in the country or up in London. Theirs remained a
formal relationship, however, as Ford's descrip-
tion of their exchanges suggests: "The politeness
of Conrad to James and of James to Conrad was one
of the most impressive kind. They always spoke
French together."[17] Another revelatory anecdote
about them is recounted by Conrad himself. Waiting
one day for James in the latter's library, he was

browsing through the books therein. When he heard James coming, however, he quickly shoved the book he was examining back on the shelf. "I didn't want to be found looking at his treasures; it might have seemed rather discourteous. He was a very charming but also a rather formidable person."[18] Since Conrad could be described as "formidable," too, their friendship tended to be more ceremonious than robust, despite their hearty mutual respect.[19]

The paths of James and Wells also crossed at frequent intervals. Given the propinquity of Rye and Sandgate, Wells could easily traipse across the Romney Marsh to spend some hours in the Lamb House garden or library, talking with "the Master." Theirs never proved to be an easy association, however, for, despite James's effort to welcome him as a fellow artist, Wells refused to accept the friendship "without some underlying resentment."[20] His cockney background, his scientific training, above all, his theories about novel writing put him at odds with James. Though each respected the other, yet, as Wells said, "I bothered him, and he bothered me." The differences between the two were too substantial--even before their famous quarrel--to permit a friendship on the order, say, of a Henry James-Edith Wharton one.

James, as one might anticipate, entertained distinct views about the literary production of his friends. His attitude toward Wells is particularly well known, his strong objection to the "orange-squeezing" saturation technique, the presentation of masses of material rather than making interesting use of the material. As Leon Edel and Gordon Ray suggest,[21] Wells's scientific training, combined with his need for self-assertion, made him an exponent of a materialistic kind of artistry to which James was utterly opposed. In spite of calling Wells the "only interesting" writer of his generation, James insisted on viewing Wells's novels by the light of his own techniques and on pressing his own theories of fiction upon him. "Strange to me," he said, ". . . the coexistence of so much talent with so little art, so much

life with (so to speak) so little living!" For
Wells, on the other hand, the novel served as a
means rather than an end in itself, and he did
not share James's insistence on a shaping form.
James, it is generally agreed, had the last word:
art makes life, makes interest, makes importance,
and there is no substitute for the beauty and
force of the process.

Unsurprisingly, James found in the very scrupulous craftsman Conrad a far more kindred soul.
"No one has known," he wrote him, on the occasion
of the appearance of The Mirror of the Sea, "for
intellectual use--the things you know, and you
have, as the artist of the whole matter, an author-
ity that no one has approached. . . . I pat you,
my dear Conrad, very affectionately and complacently on the back."22 In his essay, "The New
Novel," James praised Conrad, too, "absolutely
alone as a votary of the way to do a thing that
shall make it undergo most doing," one demonstrat-
ing "a beautiful and generous mind at play." Concerned as he was with point of view, he was interested also in Conrad's use of Marlow, the latter's
role being, in Chance, a "prolonged hovering flight
of the subjective over the outstretched ground of
the case exposed."23

James felt admiration for the talent of
Stephen Crane, too. Content to overlook the
latter's use of subjects and techniques quite
dissimilar from his own, he spoke highly of "his
dry junior 'so truly gifted,' 'of the most charming sensitiveness,' 'so very lovable.'"24 Though
perhaps Crane "never kept a Jamesian notebook,
wrote an introduction, nor (after his second
novel), employed the painter's sponge,"25 he was
as dedicated to artistic performance as was
James, and this the "ceremonial Master" recognized. Having praised The Red Badge of Courage,
appearing early in Crane's career, he was still
extending praise when the career so abruptly
closed. As he commented sadly on this "unnecessary extinction,"26 he surely had in mind the loss
of Crane's potential. It seems natural to suppose
that James approved of Crane's experimentation

with point of view, his avoidance of fully detailed plots, his psychological approach to character, and, sometimes, his choice of subject matter (the Civil War, if not the Bowery slums), and we know for certain that he often spoke--vaguely, perhaps, but firmly--of Crane's "genius."

About the work of Ford Madox Ford, James did not have much to say. They exchanged letters about a possible conflict of subject for books that each was planning, with James graciously declaring, "Go on with yours never dreaming of my job,"[27] and James occasionally let fall a remark about Ford (he did not, for one thing, approve of Ford's collaborating with Conrad).[28] According to Ford, however, theirs was a "wholly non-literary intimacy,"[29] with James never talking of books, when they met, and only sometimes about the personalities of writers, and ". . . though I walked with and listened to the Master day after day, I remember only one occasion on which he made a remark that was a revelation of his own aims and methods."[30] It should be remembered that, at the time when their friendship flourished, Ford had not yet produced his best novels, and those that could have come to James's attention presumably did not interest him very much--even if some of them were Jamesian imitations![31] As Ford himself ruefully said, ". . . I do not think that, till the end of his days, he regarded me as a serious writer."[32]

* * * * *

Joseph Conrad may safely be designated a more integral member of the "circle" than James, his friendships with Ford and Crane in particular being more intense than any that James shared with members of the group. Though described by some as shy and reclusive, in truth, "his greatest pleasure was his friends,"[33] and these included a large assortment from the literary world, Crane and Ford and James and Wells (but not Frederic), together with Galsworthy, W.H. Hudson, Cunninghame Graham,

8

the Garnetts, and others. As his no doubt preju-
diced wife declared, "Those of his friends who
knew him intimately felt his charm, and even
acquaintances came at once under his spell."[34]
His occasional gloomy states of mind notwithstanding, Conrad "always seems to have been very so-
ciable and to have enjoyed conversations . . . and
[he] had high standards of hospitality."[35]

Jessie Conrad speaks of her husband's meetings with Henry James, as also of the latter's
sending a copy of The Spoils of Poynton to Conrad,
with a touching inscription on the flyleaf,[36] and
Borys Conrad has also recalled occasional visits
to James at Rye, just fourteen miles away from
their home, Pent Farm (though young Borys's impressions of "Uncle Jack" Galsworthy seem to have
been more vivid than those of sitting on James's
knee while the latter talked and talked).[37]

The association with Wells was also pleasant,
Wells taking visitors like Shaw and Gissing to the
Pent, exchanging letters with Conrad, and extending the hospitality of his home to Joseph and
Jessie ("we spent many very happy days in . . .
Spade House").[38] If Lewis Hind, sitting with the
two writers, found "H.G.'s intriguing manner with
a touch of asperity such a contrast to Conrad's
virility and violence of utterance," he neverthe-
less saw the bond of congeniality and mutual
respect uniting them.[39]

The Conrad-Crane linking, though necessarily
of short duration because of the latter's untimely
death, proved a firm one indeed, as Jessie Conrad
attests with her comment about the "extreme good
fellowship and complete understanding between the
two artists."[40] Many visits between the nearby
homes of Pent Farm and Brede Place were exchanged,
the Conrads seemingly enjoying the colorful confu-
sion of Brede, the Cranes liking the quieter Pent,
the baby Borys, Jessie's good cooking. If something of the disciple-master relationship existed
in the friendship (Jocelyn Baines says that "Crane
seems quickly to have developed a hero-worship of

Conrad. James Huneker has said that Crane used to speak of him 'as if he were the B.V.M.'"),[41] still, it involved a genuine "liking" on both sides. Edward Garnett remembered how Conrad was "delightfully sunny and bantered 'poor Stevie' in the gentlest, most affectionate style. . . . I can still hear the shades of Crane's poignant friendliness in his cry 'Joseph!' And Conrad's delight in Crane's personality glowed in the shining warmth of his brown eyes."[42] A brief note from Crane to Conrad perhaps catches this mutual affection best: "Dear old Pard, Right. Bully for you. You are the greatest of the boys . . ."[43]

The much longer-lasting Conrad-Ford association pursued a less even course, being, for one thing, perpetually jeopardized by Mrs. Conrad's hostility toward Ford (e.g., "F.M.H. had come to the fore once more, much to my dismay, and he reverted to his old habit of treating our home as if it were one of his own").[44] Despite Ford's constant admiration of Conrad's work and unquestioned devotion to the man, the friendship had its ups and downs, Conrad being occasionally prickly and moody, Ford being almost always difficult, wittingly or otherwise. One does well to remember, however, Conrad's comment in a letter to Wells: "As to Ford he is a sort of life-long habit of which I am not ashamed because he is a much better fellow than the world gives him credit for."[45]

Conrad's reputation, in the years when this literary circle flourished, was, like that of James, not extraordinarily high, but--again like James--he was thoroughly respected by his fellow writers, and his example of craftsmanship exerted an influence (the example, if not the technique per se) upon them. Wells, as might be anticipated, was least impressed, linking Conrad with the Jamesian "aesthetics" cause. Conrad showed more charity toward "H.G.," writing to thank him, for example, for a not altogether flattering review of An Outcast of the Islands, and speaking elsewhere of how he "cannot have enough of your work."[46]

10

Other letters praise "the logic of your imagination so unbounded and so brilliant," describe The Invisible Man as "uncommonly fine," call Wells "the one honest thinker of the day,' and pray that Wells may continue "many, many years this work of making us think and feel while we are amused." Conrad could not accept, however, Wells's unconcern about novelistic technique, nor his unabashed use of fiction to disseminate his ideas on various topics of the day. They differed, finally, in their view of human nature. As Conrad put it, "The difference between us, Wells, is fundamental. You don't care for humanity but think they are to be improved. I love humanity but know they are not."[47]

James, Conrad's senior by fifteen years, and one with a long line of books to his credit before Conrad had written one, was hardly prepared to be influenced by Conrad, nor, on the other hand, did Conrad intend to take lessons from James. A high degree of artistic sympathy existed between them, however (q.v., James's "I read you as I listen to rare music"),[48] and each read the other's work with interest and appreciation. Sharing a keen regard for technique and an interest in the psychology of character, yet they differed in their choices of settings and--usually--situations, and James's scenic method probably lent to his work a less diffused focus than is sometimes found in Conrad. Both men employed distinctive styles, too, of course, though hardly comparable ones.

The closer Conrad-Crane connection might more readily have made for cross-influence. Conrad, we know, was particularly attracted by Crane's "impressionism" ("He certainly is the impressionist. . . . Why is he not immensely popular?"),[49] and it has been suggested that his reading of The Red Badge of Courage might have led him to write his own possibly-to-be-considered "impressionistic" The Nigger of the Narcissus.[50] Though finding some faults in Crane ("The man sees the outside of many things and the inside of some"),[51] Conrad essentially offered a very hearty endorsement. Crane reciprocated with strong praise of his older friend. He declared, for example, that <u>The Nigger</u> was "simply great," the death of James Wait

> too good, too terrible. . . . It caught me very hard. I felt ill over that red thread lining from the corner of the man's mouth to his chin. . . . By such small means does the real writer suddenly flash out in the sky above those who are always doing rather well.[52]

The writers clearly had much in common, an interest in the adventure format, the presentation of characters in moments of crisis, the precise selection of details, and a scrupulous attention to matters of style. They even thought about the possibility of a collaboration.[53]

The collaborative effort was left for the Conrad-Ford duo, however, and it is the literary relationship of these two members of the circle that gives the clearest evidence--and even that, muted--of mutual influence. The men wrote two novels jointly, <u>The Inheritors</u> (1901) and <u>Romance</u> (1903), together with a long short story, "The Nature of a Crime." If these tales of wild adventure contain Conradian touches, e.g., colorful imagery and rhetorical dialogue, they seem primarily the work of Ford, who had originally planned them.[54] In any case, the ventures do not threaten to emulate the efforts of more notable writing combinations like that of Beaumont and Fletcher, Addison and Steele, even Nordhoff and Hall.

Critics have declared that Conrad proposed the collaboration, needing the money that would come from book publication (and the then popular Ford probably seemed sure of sales), and also wishing for some help with his style--the English-as-his-third-language problem. Ford's reasons for joining forces are less clear, though, to be sure, he admired Conrad and found much common ground between them. His later "remembrance" of Conrad speaks of

12

how the associative effort would afford him "the pleasure of eternal technical discussion,"[55] a prospect that he admits gave him more comfort than it did Conrad. It is amusing to note that Conrad felt called upon to announce their intended collaboration to Wells, who promptly advised Ford against collaborating on the grounds that Ford would spoil Conrad's style.[56]

If the end product of their collaboration, the novels and story, does not overly impress, their necessarily intimate association during the writing and the resultant "eternal technical discussion" did lead to something of value. As Hugh Kenner puts it,

> . . . technique seduced them because it was important; no one but Henry James in those years, understood its claims so clearly; almost alone they had to redeem the English novel for the intelligent world. They did that, and they wrote memorable pages. . . . It was no small achievement to maintain an artistic conscience in Balfour's England, to wrestle in those times of facile writing with the exact enduring word.[57]

In their frequent meetings during the collaborative years, the two men theorized extensively about the art of fiction, discussing such matters as the tension between aesthetic and activist impulses—inevitably championing the former and leaving the latter for Wells—the need for an indirect method of presentation of one's material, for patterns of imagery, and for themes stemming from a probing of man seen in relationship to his environment. Ford, in his Conrad memoir, has much to say about their theories, all based on the belief that "the writing of novels was the one thing of importance that remained in the world, and that what the novel needed was the New Form."[58] They agreed on many aspects of the craft: the

13

introduction of a character into a work of fiction
with a strong impression "and then working back-
wards and forwards over his past"; the employment
of a deliberate indefiniteness (the allusions, the
unfinished sentences of all human conversations);
opposition to tacking a moral on to one's fables;
decided adherence to Conrad's famous "above all
things to make you see" dictum. They asserted,
too, that the whole of art consists in selection,
the element of surprise lends much interest, expo-
sition and "plants" must be unobtrusively inserted,
word choice should be appropriate (words that are
too startling are as fatiguing as over-used words
and jog-trot cadences), the structural pattern
must have a sense of inevitability, a "progression
d'effet"--increasing the intensity as the story
proceeds--should be utilized, and a stylistic
"cadence" should be sought. Their not numerous
disagreements included a difference of opinion
about a story's opening, Conrad seeking something
strongly dramatic whereas Ford preferred a more
"pensive approach."59 Again, Conrad objected to
repeated "he said's" in dialogue, a practice that
did not bother Ford. Mostly, they harmonized, and
to an immense degree, as they vigorously champi-
oned the novel form ("absolutely the only vehicle
for the thought of our day. With the novel you
can do anything").60

     Ford remained close to Conrad (Jessie Conrad's
antagonism notwithstanding) for a number of years
after their specific collaborations ceased, their
intimacy being resumed for a while in 1908 (until
a quarrel about Conrad's reminiscences, being written for the Ford-edited English Review, caused an
estrangement). Never put off, apparently, by
Conrad's gloomy moods, or his dilatoriness in writing his share of their joint efforts, Ford regarded
him with both affection and awe always ("how immensely strong an impression this beautiful genius
made on a mind not vastly impressionable or prone
to forming affections";61 "his achievements had
all such permanence as is vouchsafed to us men").62
And their ideas about the craft of fiction were

14

jointly employed, as jointly shared, even if the individual end results bore only moderate resemblance, one to the other.

* * * * *

Seemingly the least likely member of a literary circle--when one remembers his manifold science-oriented interests as well as his occasional "spasms of truculence"[63] toward "litt'ry" types-- was H.G. Wells. Yet Wells was drawn to the Sussex coterie (saving its Surrey member, Mr. Frederic), and for a number of reasons: physical proximity, a common interest in literature, even business arrangements (e.g., Ford was to serialize his Tono-Bungay in the English Review). He was in turn recognized by them as a major talent and was liked as well as respected.

He particularly admired Crane, that "lean, blond slow-speaking, perceptive, fragile tuberculous being, too adventurous to be temperate with anything and impracticable to an extreme degree."[64] Both Wells and his wife enjoyed the "gay extravagance and open hospitality" of Brede Place, Wells later recalling such events as the famous Christmas party, out of which came the multi-authored play whose roster of "composers" was as dazzling as the play was not. Wells saw Crane's life as, at that stage, out of control, his illness wasting him and money problems besetting him. He was, however, as a writer, "still clinging to his artistry,"[65] still producing his "admirable bare prose."

Ford and Conrad presented, in Wells's mind, the "ideal of pure artistry rather less congenially."[66] Of Ford he remarked, "What he is really or if he is really, nobody knows now and he least of all."[67] This ambiguous remark may have been provoked by Wells's irritation at Ford's casual handling of editorial responsibilities; in any event it seems directed more at the man than at the author. With Conrad, Wells enjoyed a "long, fairly friendly but always strained acquaintance.

15

. . . I think he found me Philistine, stupid and intensely English; he was incredulous that I could take social and political issues seriously."68 Although appreciative of Conrad's rich descriptive prose, Wells felt that the exotic style could not always hide the essentially sentimental and melo- dramatic character of the stories he told, and they grew further apart in their literary views-- if not in their friendly association--as Conrad complained about Wells's sociological preoccupa- tions and his zeal for reform, and as Wells de- plored Conrad's having "gone literary with a singleness and intensity of purpose that made the kindred concentration of Henry James seem lax and large and pale."69

The James-Wells friendship followed a rather similar pattern, being "sincere but troubled. . . . We were by nature and training profoundly unsympa- thetic."70 The blunt cockney in Wells could never understand James's extreme fastidiousness (why shouldn't William James climb up a wall to peek at G.K. Chesterton?), nor could he, finally, accept the Jamesian dictum that "it is art that makes life." Still, the mutual appreciation lingered-- "your amazing skill in atmosphere," said Wells of A Small Boy and Others,71 "a bloody little chunk of life," said James of Love and Mr. Lewisham72-- at least, until the Boon incident.

Certainly we are offered some pleasant glimpses of Wells's association with the circle, accounts not only of the "larky" parties at Brede Place but also of jolly gatherings at Wells's own home. Jessie Conrad, for one, spoke of the "un- varying kindness and hospitality we always found" at Spade House,73 and the host himself later re- called the entertainment offered, especially the dramas improvised by his wife and participated in by such as Ford Madox Ford, posing as a "croupier at a green table in a marvellous Monte Carlo scene."74 We hear also of Wells's frequent treks to Lamb House, often having in tow writers like George Gissing, who wanted to meet James--a "lion" to his fellow authors if not to the general public.

There was, in short, a "good deal of weekend entertaining. . . . much coming and going,"[75] with Wells
(the "best company in the world" when he was not
being mean, spiteful and quarrelsome!),[76] often at
the center of the stage.

The rub usually came when Wells introduced his
views on literary matters, views so very much at
odds, basically, with those of his friends. Talk
about "le mot juste," "rendering" impressions,
"point of view" did not really seem important to
Wells, and "in the end I revolted altogether and
refused to play their game."[77] Before the revolt,
to be sure, Wells had given substantial evidence
of his interest in the craft of fiction[78] as well
as of his own skill as a novelist. The "Dickensi-
an" novels which James and a number of others much
admired[79] had been carefully composed and gave
firm testimony to his skill as a story-teller, his
imagination and his comic sense. Turning, after
1910, however, more and more to the "novel of
discussion," he grew careless about technique,
tending to forget the "novelist" in the "reformer."
It was then that he instituted a series of denials
of artistic intent in his work, declaring with
belligerence, "I am a journalist, not an artist."
His insistence on the use of fiction to propagan-
dize for his ideas, his subordinating characters
to the particular problems with which their lives
were involved, his shifts in point of view (a
digression or ironical aside could further the
propaganda and hence they were perfectly permis-
sible), his undemandingness with regard to style--
these were, of course, anathema to Ford and James
and Conrad.[80] Along with a semi-pamphlet war
(e.g., Wells's "The Contemporary Novel," James's
"The Younger Generation"), came letter exchanges
among them. Though sometimes apologetic ("That
book is gawky. . . . I shall never be an artist.
My art is abortion," "I agree about the first
person. The only artistic 'first person' is the
onlooker speculative 'first person,' and God helping me, this shall be the last young gushing Hari-
Karis"),[81] Wells more often took the offensive,
pounding home his message that the novelist's

17

business was to journalize life; the ideas being preeminent, art must take a secondary role. Thus, he came to dispense with carefully drawn characters and used the 'exponent character' that he had earlier deplored.[82] Thus, he chose to be a philosopher masquerading as novelist, a role he had earlier opposed. Thus, he insisted upon a thoroughly functional style ("I write as straight as I can, because that is the best way to get there").[83]

His antipathy toward those who would persuade him of the imperativeness of subtlety and artistry in novel-writing came to a climax in the "quarrel" with James. As he put it, in response to James's reaction to the pamphlet Boon,

I have a natural horror of dignity,
finish and perfection, a horror a little
enhanced by theory. You may take it
that my sparring and punching at you is
very much due to the feeling that you
were 'coming over' me, and that if I was
not very careful I should find myself
giving way altogether to respect. There
is of course a real and very fundamental
difference in our innate and developed
attitudes towards life and literature.
To you literature like painting is an
end, to me literature like architecture
is a means, it has a use. Your view was,
I felt, altogether too dominant in the
world of criticism, and I assailed it in
tones of harsh antagonism. . . . I had
rather be called a journalist than an
artist, that is the essence of it, and
there was no other antagonist possible
than yourself. But since it was printed
I have regretted a hundred times that I
did not express our profound and incur-
able difference and contrast with a better
grace. And believe me, my dear James,
your very keenly appreciative reader,
your warm if rebellious and resentful

admirer, and for countless causes yours most gratefully and affectionately....[84]

James's second reply simply declared, "I am bound to tell you that I don't think your letter makes any sort of case for the bad manners of <u>Boon</u> so far as your indulgence in them at the expense of your poor old H.J. is concerned."[85] The "bad manners" issue aside, it is worth remarking that Wells retained all of James's letters to him and may have stowed away in some corner of his still partially artistic soul the precepts contained therein ("the crucible of the imagination . . . the observant and recording and interpreting mind" playing its part, ". . . the fictional form . . . opens such widely different windows of attention").[86] One recent critic has gone so far as to say that <u>between</u> them "Wells and James profoundly influenced the modern novel,"[87] perhaps regarding, as Wells's major contribution, the "convulsed with life" quality that James himself praised.[88]

As the reputations of the other members of the circle have advanced in the twentieth century, ironically, that of Wells, so immense in the early years of the century, has rather abruptly declined. Though still admired for his gay social comedies like <u>Love and Mr. Lewisham</u>, <u>Kipps</u>, <u>Tono-Bungay</u> and <u>The History of Mr. Polly</u>, and respected as a pioneer in science fiction, Wells is more readily regarded as a "personage," a remarkably alert and colorful individual, than as a novelist of stature. His influence, strong in his own time (on such as Bennett and Gissing, if not on James and Conrad), has very much abated, his example proving--as he himself anticipated--the dangers of topicality, of confusing art with propaganda. Yet, just as the affection of James for "this touchy, perverse little artist . . . never wavered,"[89] so, too, that of a surprisingly large number of readers. These turn to his books--some of them--not put off by his monologuist characters (whom he sometimes elbowed aside to discourse on his own), nor by his all-

brains-and-very-little-heart persona (as reflected
in his so often harsh comments about his con-
freres), and they seem to find him an exhilarating
force and a stimulating thinker, one, too, who was
surely as cosmopolitan as any of his Sussex associates, possessed of a comprehensive "world" view.

* * * * *

The name of the long-neglected Ford now runs
through the fabric of the modern novel, with certain of his books highly acclaimed, as they should
be, and with his corpus being subjected to an
overdue thorough scrutiny. "At his best," says
one critic, "Ford is superior to Conrad because he
is, by lengths, the finer artist. The work of his
one-time collaborator is, in fact, peculiarly
heavy."[90] And again: "James's deficiency as com-
pared with Ford is not his art but the limited
depth of emotion in his work."[91] If such comments
might easily lead to an over-redressing of the
balance, yet the reputation of Ford deserves en-
hancing, The Good Soldier and Parade's End serving
as major contributions to twentieth century literature. It seems fitting that the generosity which
he himself bestowed on so many writers, especially
aspiring ones ("Only Uncle of the Gifted Young,"
Wells called him as early as 1915),[92] has, at
length, come home to roost.

Ford may probably be called the most eager
participant in the literary circle with which we
are concerned, a collaborator with Conrad, a wor-
shipper of James, a genuine admirer of Crane, an
off-and-on friend of Wells, even an occasional
associate of Frederic. His playing such a role
seems fitting, given his faith that literature
needed behind it some "cohesion of writers."[93]
Citing the Pre-Raphaelite Brotherhood, the
"Flaubert group," and the "Henley gang" as prece-
dents, Ford chose to believe in "cohesive art move-
ments after the French fashion"[94] and felt, for a
time at least, that the set of writers living near
each other in the south of England might constitute

a group with a similar position with regard to literary method. And so perhaps they did, the early deaths and scant theorizing of Frederic and Crane, and the post-1910 dissenting opinion of Wells notwithstanding.

About Ford's association with the group we hear a great deal, especially in his countless memoirs and reminiscences. These volumes, Thus to Revisit, Return to Yesterday, Mightier than the Sword, Ancient Lights, It Was the Nightingale, provide fascinating reading, though one always has to bear in mind that Ford's "unreliability and his disregard for consistence are notorious."[95] To this, one should no doubt add another caveat, the difficulty to be found in penetrating Ford's various guises and masks and contradictory identities; one remembers Wells's warning, "What he is really or if he is really, nobody knows now and he least of all." An alternately very charming and very irritating man, he inspired among his contemporaries both intense loyalties and intense antagonisms. If one could take him in stride, laughing off his eccentricities, as did Crane ("He patronizes Mr. James. He patronizes Mr. Conrad. Of course he patronizes me and he will patronize Almighty God when they meet, but God will get used to it, for Hueffer is all right!"),[96] such was the best course.

The Ford-Frederic conjunction was brief and not very important. Crane had presumably brought them together at his first English home, Ravensbrook in Oxted, and they may also have met in London, perhaps through the aegis of Violet Hunt.[97] Ford's comments on Frederic and his work are not, however, easily to be found;[98] he was much more preoccupied with Frederic's fellow countrymen W.H. Hudson and Stephen Crane, both of whom he deeply admired.

On the subject of "poor Steevie" Ford could wax eloquent. "For me, Crane came nearer to the otherworldly being than any human soul I have ever encountered."[99] Introduced to one another by

Edward Garnett, they enjoyed frequent exchanges of visits when Crane lived at Oxted and Ford nearby im Limpsfield. Ford would willingly help Cora Crane with dressmaking "of the medieval variety," then much more willingly discuss literature with Crane into the early morning hours. Beneath the latter's "harsh and defiant surface" and vocabulary of the "Man of Action of dime drama," Ford discerned the poet and the "impressionistic" novelist. After the Cranes were settled at Brede Place, the two men continued to meet, and Ford continued to regard Crane very highly, "an Apollo with starry eyes,"[100] honorable, physically brave, infinitely hopeful, generous and morally courageous. The "rave notices" extended to Crane's writing as well. He was, according to Ford, the "first really American writer"--because the first to be passionately interested in the life that surrounded him.[101]

Ford's "impressionist memories" include glimpses of Crane in association with their mutual neighbor Henry James, toward whom Steevie was "boyishly respectful and enthusiastic."[102] The respect could, to be sure, be tempered with some teasing, Crane delighting in assuming his "Bowery cloak" or a cowboy role in some of his appearances at Lamb House. If James was perplexed by these personae, yet "from Steevie he had stood and would have stood a great deal more."[103] Ford also notes that the two men, as far as he knew, did not discuss literary matters with one another, perhaps silently recognizing their essentially disparate approaches to writing.

It seems a little more surprising, given their permeating interest in matters of technique, that Ford and James also had a "wholly non-literary intimacy."[104] During their almost daily meetings at teatime, when Ford was living in Winchelsea, a scant four miles from Rye, they talked and talked-- but, said Ford, not of books, and only occasionally of the personalities of writers. As James, "magisterial in the manner of a police-magistrate,"[105] expressed his views about Ford's Pre-Raphaelite

Brotherhood relatives (too Bohemian in James's eyes) or Flaubert, messy in his dressing gown, Ford mostly listened, awed in the presence of this "commanding figure," who seemed to view him as a journalist rather than as a serious writer and thus may not have even thought of debating about fictional processes with him. Ford was interested in James-the-writer at any rate, always admiring his skills, indeed praising them extravagantly in an essay-tribute written in 1913. It is said that James never bothered to read this enthusiastic but superficial and even inaccurate assessment.[106]

Hardly more "lovable,"[107] than the "Grand Panjandrum" was H.G. Wells, but Ford, in a fashion more characteristic of him, did not demonstrate the same deference to Wells as to James. He could even declare, late in his life, that they had been enemies "for more years than I care now to think of."[108] This, like other Ford recollections, should be regarded with some distrust, however. The Ford-Wells relationship, first established in the late 1890s, maintained itself for many years, their quarrels--chiefly about Ford's handling of the serialization of Tono-Bungay in the English Review in 1908--notwithstanding.

Ford disagreed with Wells fundamentally on the matter of the importance of literature, believing, as he many times declared, that the world was to be saved by the Arts, not by Science, and thus associating himself with the "conscious artists" like James, Crane, Conrad, and Hudson, and criticizing Wells for immersing himself so thoroughly in public affairs and for assuming, in his novels, so didactic a tone. He could admire Wells's mind and his courage, however, and could also praise some of his fictional efforts, The Sea Lady, for one, and especially Tono-Bungay--"a really great book. It has all the qualities of the traditional classical English novel and it is much better handled than any of the British classical novels."[109]

Personal contact with Wells proved pleasurable as well, Ford regarding this "Arbiter of the

World"110 as one of the great talkers of his time.
He was also an admirer of Jane Wells and appreciated the lively parties at Spade House. The
English Review incident inevitably put a damper on
the friendship, as did also Ford's liaison with
Violet Hunt. Wells, if guilty himself of extra-
marital affairs, did not approve of the Hunt-Ford
menage, at least in its public and messy aspects.
However, meetings and correspondence between the
two men occurred well into their later years, and
long after they had ceased to live "rather in each
other's pockets,"111 they maintained a relationship of mutual respect--a respect greater on the
part of Ford than of Wells, to be sure.112

Ford, a mixture of modesty and effrontery, of
sensitivity and callousness--"I dare say I was not
a very agreeable young man"113--often experienced
difficulties in his friendships. At least one of
these, however, that with Conrad, proved firm and
lasting. Notwithstanding the fact that both "were
susceptible to the irritations and doubts that
come with artistic temperaments,"114 and that
Jessie Conrad (who was to attack Ford so vigorously after her husband's death) lurked disapproving-
ly in the background, they sustained a conjunction
clearly based on a hard core of abiding affection.
Ford loved Conrad the man ("the pleasure derived
from his society was inexhaustible"),115 and he
thoroughly admired his work ("a week after the
publication of his first book, he stood absolutely
in the front rank of English authors").116 The
two never quarreled, he said, nor felt envy of one
another. That Conrad agreed--with more reserve--
about the closeness of the bond is also attested
to: if at times in his misanthropic moods he may
have denigrated "Fordie," he also declared that
his love "is always with you."117

The companionship began in 1898, when Edward
Garnett introduced the two men, and remained an
intimate one for some ten years, nor did the
friendship really cease then. Until Conrad's
death they corresponded, if they did not meet,
with Ford's very flattering essay on Conrad, which

soon followed this event, nicely capping the association.

From the partnership stemmed their collaborative writing efforts, Romance, The Inheritors, and
"The Nature of a Crime." This harnessing of two
creative minds in joint endeavors produced moments
of discomfort as well as comfort, it must be ad-
mitted, Ford having to endure Conrad's frequent
complaints about ill health, financial problems,
and writer's block. Yet both profited from their
mutual dedication to the craft of writing and from
their innumerable discussions of novelistic technique. Theirs was, it has rightly been said, a
working relationship of equals rather than a
master-disciple affair. While Conrad set for Ford
the example of an intense passion for his art,
causing the latter to declare emphatically, ". . .
if I know anything of how to write, almost the
whole of that knowledge was acquired then,"[118]
Ford in turn supported Conrad, not only aiding him
in practical matters (e.g., in dealings with
Conrad's agent J.B. Pinker), but also strongly en-
couraging him in his belief in the novel as a most
valuable art form.

As previously mentioned, the fruits of their
joint writing leave a good deal to be desired, the
plain truth being that neither The Inheritors nor
Romance nor the "crime" story comes near the ideal
'welded' collaboration of which the authors
spoke.[119] The Inheritors (which was written almost
entirely by Ford, Conrad confining himself to some
revising and the insertion of a few of the details)[120] seems a conventional mystery melodrama
and is, as the subtitle says, "an extravagant
story," filled with tortuous intrigue. It is most
Fordian, one feels, in its laconic but sophisti-
cated and satire-tinged dialogue. With Romance
the authors hoped "to show just how vivid real
craftsmen could make even a simple adventure
story,"[121] but again they met with very indifferent
success. Conrad contributed an equal share this
time, and his portions (usually identifiable
through the style--"his face was very pale, and had

the leaden transparency of a boiled artichoke; it was fringed by a red beard streaked with gray, as brown flood-water is with foam") are generally the better. Events do not move very smoothly, however, and the style remains uneven and often strained. Since every collaboration, as Ford said, involved a "contest of temperaments,"[122] there probably could not have been a perfect meshing. One does note, in both works, the authors' mutual interests on display, for example, the employment of a first-person narrator and the presentation of a rather sardonic "world-view."

The evidence of strain in the combined undertaking notwithstanding, the collaboration did benefit both men to some degree, Conrad becoming a more flexible and fluent writer (though Ford insisted that he had no part "in teaching Conrad English"),[123] and Ford a more painstaking one ("There is not a chapter I haven't made him write twice--most of them three times over," Conrad wrote to Edward Garnett).[124] Their exchange of ideas about craft and the theory of the novel was of tremendous importance, too, in the development of both as novelists.

It is these discussions of technique, rather than the co-authored novels, that remain of interest today. The stress laid by Conrad and Ford on the novel as an art form helped pave the way for Joyce and other early twentieth century experimenters. Though some critics have accused the pair of being too beguiled by technique and have seen this emphasis as affecting their writing adversely,[125] others have found the theorizing of value, and a help rather than a hindrance to the authors' fiction.[126] Both Conrad and Ford used the "New Form" --the indirect presentation of character, integral image patterns, "progression d'effet," stylistic cadence--adroitly.

In theory as in practice they anticipated a number of "modernist" approaches, rejecting the straight narrative line, for example, in favor of complex structural arrangements involving many shifts of time. They also talked of the use of a double perspective on their material, and of employing a central event as it affected a small circle of people, with the interest focusing on subtleties in relationships among them. Much stress was laid upon "impressionism"--an ambiguous term, to be sure--and upon symbolism, and they discussed at great length the importance of vocabulary. If Ford remained a trifle less dedicated than Conrad to the Flaubertian concept of "le mot juste," still, he insisted upon meticulous word selection. What he wanted was a non-literary vocabulary, a keying down of the prose (not Elizabethanism, but a use of "our vernacular so willfully that words, precious or obsolete, will not stick out"),[127] with an easy command of English idiom as central. Both men agreed, finally, on the importance of an author's self-effacement, of an implicit rather than explicit authorial presence. Each proved an intelligent audience for the other in their mutual critical formulations, and at a time when matters of technique were often, as Ford said, "laughed to scorn,"[128] they lent dignity to the novelist and his technique and to the novel as an important cultural force.

* * * * *

The focusing figure in this "community of letters"[129] was Stephen Crane, the one so much admired and respected by all the rest. Whereas Wells could always lecture Ford, and Conrad could give him bad moments, whereas James could quarrel with Wells, ignore Ford as a writer and treat Conrad with a certain gingerliness, whereas Frederic clearly remained perched on the group's periphery, Crane neatly bound them all, discussing "words" with Ford for hours on end, helping Frederic with personal problems, persuading Wells to act in a pageant, even delighting--while sometimes puzzling--James. Constantly he crops up in their memoirs as the colorful but genuine friend and as the dedicated artist.

Nicely utilizing these memoirs, Eric Solomon, in his book Stephen Crane in England, offers some vivid glimpses of the "community" and of Crane's attachment to it. He pictures Wells grimly bicycling through the night to get a doctor for the stricken Crane, Ford conversing away while wandering around the Crane rose garden, James complacently eating a doughnut at a Cora Crane soirée, Conrad walking for hours through Hyde Park with Crane while discussing Balzac's novels, and Frederic escorting him to lunch at the Savage Club and introducing him to such as Sir James Barrie, Justin McCarthy, and Anthony Hope.

It was a circle flexible enough to accept the Cranes--American, exotic, unmarried--without question. Conrad had, as Solomon says, knocked about the world, James was a bachelor (albeit a fastidious one), Ford and Wells had their own marital problems, as certainly did Frederic with his "odd domestic arrangement of two distinct households."130

More important, it afforded Crane intellectual freedom and escape from prudish censorship, and these "literary friendships" may indeed have contributed to "his growth as an artist."131 Of the American writers he had known, those such as Richard Harding Davis and Ripley Hitchcock were hardly serious novelists, those like Garland and Howells admired his talent but tended to treat him condescendingly. With such as Conrad and James, however, he would communicate "not as a disciple to masters, but as an artist to artists, despite--perhaps because of--the obvious age differences."132 Since he was as interested as they were in new literary methods and was an equally dedicated craftsman, it is not surprising that he relished their presence and their conversation. Though his "wild young American" side, his dashing off to Cuba and Greece and elsewhere to soak up experience, may have perplexed the tidy-minded James, still, the latter was shrewd enough to recognize the equally predominant other side, the very self-conscious literary artist. James and the other

Sussex-ers obviously found Crane an attractive and interesting person, something of the "glorious boy" in the Chatterton pattern, but also the mature fictional artist. He was, as Conrad said, "one of us."[133]

Harold Frederic served, no doubt, as Crane's closest friend during his "English years," introducing him to writers and praising his genius (lauding "The Open Boat" in a New York Times review),[134] visiting him and traveling with him. To Crane he extended literary counsel, too, suggesting a mining of his own experiences rather than reliance on too fanciful an imagination. Thus placing his faith primarily in an author's "authenticity," he approved of Crane's Active Service, drawn as it was from Crane's actual observation of the Greco-Turkish War.[135] Since he by and large shared this view, Crane approved of Frederic's own realistic productions such as The Damnation of Theron Ware.

Crane did say with regard to Theron Ware that it "could have been written a darned lot better."[136] Not one to let friendship interfere with frankness, he quarreled with Frederic's appraisal of some of his (Crane's) work, refusing, for example, to throw away his story "The Monster" as Frederic recommended.[137] Still, theirs proved a congenial companionship ("many a merry night together" at Ravensbrook, as Robert Barr reported),[138] sustained until Frederic's death in 1898,[139] and it was the Cranes, chiefly Cora, who sought financial support for Frederic's widow (one of the two!) after his demise.

The nature of the relationship between Crane and James cannot be quite so easily defined. As Solomon says, "Since both Crane and James would assume masks and often present different faces to different audiences, it is difficult to trust the statements of those who observed their meetings."[140] Though there can be no doubt of James's solicitousness at the time of Crane's death ("You will have felt," he wrote to Wells, "as I have done, the

miserable sadness of poor Crane's so precipitated
and, somehow, so unnecessary extinction"),141
stresses had been earlier apparent, James put off
by such as Crane's flamboyant "western" attire
and probably never fully at ease in the presence
of his wife, and Crane, on the other hand, not too
entranced by his senior's ceremoniousness and
formal pattern of living. Their writing was of
course quite unlike in subject matter and style,
yet they seem to have recognized very precisely
each other's talents. James endorsed such efforts
as The Red Badge of Courage and "The Open Boat,"
while Crane admired The Portrait of a Lady and
What Maisie Knew.142 Some similarities in their
approach to fiction may be found, for instance, an
experimentation with point of view and an avoidance of detailed plots, but the dissimilarities
are surely more marked. Crane did not, on the
whole, share James's interest in literary theory,
though when he did voice criticisms, they made
good sense and, one feels, would have received
James's approval. The latter would surely have
agreed with Crane's praise of the adroit charac-
terization in Wells's early novels, his labelling
Tolstoy a supreme writer but too lecturing a one,
and his insistence, for a novelist, on form and
control,143 and he might even have accepted Crane's
stricture about his own story "In the Cage"--
"Women think more directly than he lets this girl
think."144 In general, James and Crane enjoyed
similar literary tastes, liking such figures as
Turgenev and Moore, disliking Stevenson and Henley.

Whatever the undercurrents in their relationship, courtesies marked the association, the flavor
of which is perhaps suggested by Crane's comment
that "it seems impossible to dislike him. He is so
kind to everybody,"145 and by James's more enthusiastic remarks quoted earlier: "so truly gifted,"
"so very lovable"--even if displaying "the manner-
isms of a Mile-End Roader."146 If one has to
accept as apocryphal the "stories" about Crane, at
a London party, rescuing James's silk hat when an
overbold young lady endeavored to pour champagne in
it, or James cowering when Crane cantered up to tea

in cowboy regalia, one accepts as true the accounts of a constant exchange of visits between
Brede Place and Lamb House and the testimonies as
to their mutual respect for each other.

Another in the coterie who rated Crane highly
--in fact, more highly than James, who perhaps
tended to see him as the gifted apprentice--was
Ford. Accepting Crane as a dedicated artist im-
mediately upon knowing him and his work, Ford continued to express this opinion many, many years
later. For him Crane represented a change from
the standard novel tradition, and he admired such
qualities in the American as his selective technique (the "less is more" principle), interest in
words, and employment of a kaleidoscopic imagery.
Crane belonged, Ford felt, in that "new novel"
group of Conrad, James and Ford himself, with, of
course, that other famous "member from Sussex,"
Wells, the practitioner of the novel of saturation
rather than of selection, excluded. From his talks
with "Steevie" as well as from his reading of the
Crane corpus, Ford knew of their mutual interest
in an author's remaining objective and refusing to
moralize, in his "rendering" rather than telling,
in his focusing, whatever the actual subject matter, on the "human condition." As Solomon puts it,
"Ford understood Crane's artistry. Crane was the
equal in intent and partial achievement of Henry
James and Joseph Conrad."[147]

Ford, among the first to flock to the Cranes'
Thursday open-houses at Ravensbrook, and later an
occasional visitor at Brede, particularly appreciated the opportunity to exchange with Crane ideas
about the craft of fiction, and about fellow
writers, contemporary or otherwise. Though his
reminiscences tend to convey but a general impression, Crane as the "beautiful genius" sort of
thing, they do also give more precise glimpses on
occasion, e.g., Ford's recognition of Crane's
accurate observation of the New York slums, of his
penchant for the adventure format, used, however,
to unfold moral scruples or the lack of same, and
of his disillusioned tone. Ford also gave him

31

credit for discovering and giving a "voice to America,"148 a faulty assessment chronologically but an interesting reflection coming at a time when English writers were usually deploring or ignoring--still--the "native" American strain.

As to what Crane thought of Ford and his work, we have little if any record. He obviously found the latter a stimulating conversationalist and was attracted to his theories about the "new novel," and, tolerant and "large" as he was, he could see that Ford as a person, behind the many not always appealing facades, was, as we have quoted before, "all right."

H.G. Wells, in reminiscences no doubt more reliable than those of Ford, left a clear impression of the fascination that Crane exerted upon him, both as a person and as a writer. The individual, whether violent in the saddle or quiet at a party, charmed him, and he found Crane's work to be tightly written and full of novelty, particularly The Open Boat collection of short stories which appeared in 1898. When he reviewed Crane's work in an article for the North American Review in 1900, he underlined the author's persistent selection of the essential elements of an impression and ruthless exclusion of mere information. Novels like Maggie and George's Mother demonstrated, he said, a compulsion of sympathy; stories like "The Open Boat" and "The Wise Men" were powerful yet restrained; in The Red Badge of Courage the chromatic splashes were less controlled, and The Third Violet seemed effective only in parts. In sum, Wells declared that "when at last the true proportions can be seen, Crane will be found to occupy a position singularly cardinal. . . . He began stark [and was] the first expression of the opening mind of a new period."149

The defense of Crane as a self-conscious craftsman contains its startling aspects, first as coming from Wells, and second as running counter to the prevailing contemporary view. It should be remembered with regard to the first that Wells, in

1900, did support structure and design in fiction,[150] even if he was soon to substitute claims of polemicism for those of craft. It should be remembered with regard to the second that the picture of Crane as a slapdash, intuitive kind of writer was an incorrect assessment.[151] Eric Solomon puts it more accurately in stating that "Crane, while in England, was diligently working through problems of the art of fiction--just as, elsewhere in the rolling Surrey [sic] hills, James, Ford and Conrad were seeking new approaches to fictional representation."[152]

Wells continued his efforts in later years to build up Crane's reputation (even in Boon, where he was at the same time busily assailing the other Sussex associates, James, Conrad and Ford). Mindful of Crane as a stout friend and pleasant comrade during their few months of association, and still regretting his untimely death, he spoke, as late as 1934, in glowing terms of this "very important acquaintance."[153] Though Crane's life may have gone out of control, Wells said of that last year, he clung to his artistry, and Wells felt that his "ample fiction" would not die, there being an "essential greatness" to his work.[154]

About the closeness of the Conrad-Crane bond there can be no doubt, a high degree of mutual respect, "based on art as well as personality,"[155] existing between them. Even before they had met one another, they had admired each other's work, e.g., Crane bestowing accolades on The Nigger of the Narcissus as did Conrad on The Red Badge of Courage, and in the days when they lived in conjunction, they vacationed together, talking of sharing a house (or, at least, a boat) and of collaborating on a play. After Crane's death Conrad joined the group of people who endeavored to keep his memory alive and to foster his reputation. He had found in the younger American a brooding visionary who shared his heart of darkness, and to him he offered respect as well as personal warmth.

Not that Conrad failed to perceive the limitations of his confrere, knowing as well as did Ford and Wells of the disorganized domestic scene at Brede, and recognizing along with Edward Garnett that Crane was writing too hurriedly in his last years. However, he found nothing but merit in The Open Boat collection of stories, especially "The Price of the Harness," and, if he did not consider him to be the finest writer of that generation--which was Crane's view of Conrad --he often called attention to Crane's many literary skills.

The two men were sometimes linked together in the public eye at the time of their association, and indeed parallels exist between them. Both sought to base their fiction on an organic structure, for example, to employ precise phrasing, to "render" a story rather than just to tell it, to rely on suggestive impressions, and to create a distinct atmosphere. Both focused their work on moral dilemmas, being concerned with the often tangled motives of their characters, and developing their themes by means of irony and symbolism. Both deployed their men-of-action protagonists against exotic, or at least far from prosaic, backgrounds. They differed in some ways, to be sure, with Crane avoiding for the most part the multiple points of view and manifold time shifts of Conrad and certainly offering a simplified version of Conrad's luxuriant style.

The friendship had begun in 1897 and remained an intense one until Crane's death. When not enjoying "long powwows"[156] face to face, the two writers exchanged letters, sometimes discussing each other's work (Conrad, for example, on "The Harness" as "the best bit of work you've done (for its size) since the Red Badge"),[157] sometimes confining themselves to matters domestic and personal. While Conrad worried about Crane's increasing debts, Crane seemed to ignore them, or prefer, anyway, to talk about the Conrads' baby Borys or about plans for get-togethers.

34

They were clearly bound by natural affinities, both expatriates, both rather impoverished and rather ill (though in Crane's case no hypochondria was involved), and, far more important, both entertaining an essentially nihilistic vision of the universe. Their ironic approach to life's moral dilemmas can so often be glimpsed in their fiction, e.g., the theme of cowardice, the role of chance, the harshness of nature, even the anti-imperialistic note. They shared as well, of course, a devotion to the craft of fiction, and, though Conrad surpassed Crane as an artist overall, the latter, in the originality of his technique, probably contributed as much to the course of twentieth century fiction.

Conrad often wrote appreciatively about his friend in the years following the latter's death. A wonderful artist whenever he took his pen in hand, said Conrad, "and his passage on this earth was like that of a horseman riding swiftly in the dawn of a day fated to be short and without sunshine."158 Such glowing comments attested to Conrad's deep affection for his American friend. If he sometimes qualified his praise (tending, e.g., to agree with Edward Garnett that Crane had "peaked" early as a writer and that he could be a careless practitioner), his reservations were remarkably few, and he chose to view his neighbor and companion as a concerned and skillful writer.

The "equable glow, morally and temperamentally"159 that bound Conrad and Crane in essence linked the others in the circle as well. Specific instances of the influencing process are, as aforesaid, difficult to ascertain; the resemblances between Crane's "The Open Boat" and Conrad's "Youth," for example, seem most easily explained as fortuitous. The evidence of an Anglo-American interchange is likewise slim. Crane and Frederic did not impinge of the English literary consciousness so much because· of their employment of American materials as because of their technical proficiency, and all the members of the group, with the possible exception of Wells, felt more inclined to European roots (e.g., Flaubert, Turgenev) than to specifically English or American ones. Nonetheless, the summation of Samuel Hynes with regard to what he calls the "Rye Revolutionists" seems defensible: "Important English writers do not ordinarily fit very neatly into schools, but the Rye Revolutionists were, in a loose way, a kind of school, held together by common theories about fiction, by common likes and dislikes. . . ."160

Beyond a doubt the novelists, barring Wells, looked upon fiction as a noble calling and the perfection of its art as all important. They accepted Ford's view that art was "the only real and permanent salvation of mankind" and the artist the ideal sensitized instrument recording the "truth,"161 and they agreed, again with the exception of Wells, about the importance of such matters as the selective impression, a suitable and carefully designed style, and the application of one's own moral vision to a phase of life (whether it be Conrad's sea or Crane's slums did not matter).

It is really no wonder that they all got along so famously, sharing theories, interests, even, for the most part, temperaments. James of course would not be caught twanging the guitar and singing Neapolitan airs as Crane was fond of doing, Conrad probably refused to join in the Wells-invented game of racing on broomsticks over the polished floor at Brede Place, and neither Ford nor Frederic would have been as worried as James that Cora Crane might sneak an actress or two into her house-parties there.162 Still, consanguinity accompanied the propinquity, and, most significant from the point of view of literary history, their work prospered during the period of their association. Each author--possibly because of the stimulus provided by the proximity of his peers--offered valuable contributions to the canons of fiction. For this we can be grateful for the temporary "colonizing" of the "Rye Revolutionists."163

FOOTNOTES

[1]Stanley Weintraub, The London Yankees (New
York: Harcourt Brace, Jovanovich, 1979), p. 148.

[2]Whether present in person or not, they contributed to the gatherings, James, Conrad, and
Wells lending a hand, for example, in the composi-
tion of the "ghost" play which was a major feature
of the Christmas party of 1899. (See John D.
Gordan, "The Ghost at Brede Place," Bulletin of
the New York Public Library, 56 [December, 1952],
591-595.)

[3]One notes John Berryman's comment about
James, Crane and Conrad: "Nothing could be stranger
than this close relation, within a few Sussex miles
of each other, of two Americans who were making
ready Twentieth Century prose in English, with
nearby in Essex a Pole the friend of both, who
learned from both, their solitary peer in art
though not in originality. Art likes these junc-
tures. . . ." (John Berryman, Stephen Crane [New
York: William Sloane Associates, 1950], p. 252).

[4]Crane himself said that Frederic, even after
fourteen years in England, remained "with no gild-
ing, no varnish, a great reminiscent panorama of
the Mohawk Valley." (Stephen Crane, "Harold
Frederic," The Chicago Chapbook, VIII, 1898, 358).
To be sure, Crane clung to his own upper New
Jersey antecedents, or at least did not become
distinctly Anglicized.

[5]See Rupert Hart-Davis, Hugh Walpole (New
York: MacMillan, 1952), p. 179.

[6]Thomas Beer, Stephen Crane (Garden City, N.Y.:
Garden City Publishing Company, Inc., 1927), pp.
151-152.

[7]James recognized the aristocracy's hypocrisy and anti-intellectualism, of course--quite as clearly as did Frederic.

[8]See Austin Briggs, Jr., _The Novels of Harold Frederic_ (Ithaca and London: Cornell University Press, 1969), p. 8.

[9]Crane, op. cit., 359.

[10]"The two novelists and their mistresses were companions, frequenting each other's homes and vacationing together in Ireland." It was Frederic's "only intimate literary association" (Stanton Garner, _Harold Frederic_ [Minneapolis: University of Minnesota Press, 1969], p. 39).

[11]Jean Frantz Blackall, "Frederic's _Gloria Mundi_ as a Novel of Education," _The Markham Review_, 3 (May, 1972), 41.

[12]Lillian B. Gilkes, "Stephen Crane and the Harold Frederics," _The Serif_, 6 (December, 1969), 48.

[13]Lillian Gilkes hazards the notion that Frederic's _The Return of the O'Mahony_ sparked Crane's _The O'Ruddy_ (in her article "The Third Violet, _Active Service_ and _The O'Ruddy_: Stephen Crane's Potboilers," included in _Stephen Crane in Transition_, edited by Joseph Katz [DeKalb, Illinois: Northern Illinois University Press, 1972], pp. 120-121), and, to be sure, there are many similarities between the two books.

[14]Gertrude Atherton, "The American Novel in England," _Bookman_, 30 (1910), 633.

[15]Quoted in Leon Edel, ed., _The Selected Letters of Henry James_ (New York: Farrar, Straus & Cudahy, 1955), p. xx.

[16]Ford Madox Ford, _Return to Yesterday_ (New York: Horace Liveright, Inc., 1932), p. 205.

[17] Michael Killigrew, ed., Your Mirror to My Times (The Selected Autobiographies and Impressions of Ford Madox Ford) (New York: Holt, Rinehart, Winston, 1971), p. 126.

[18] Joseph Conrad, A Sketch (Garden City, N.Y.: Doubleday Page & Co., 1924), pp. 25-26.

[19] A full account of this friendship is given by Elsa Nettels in her James and Conrad (Athens, Georgia: University of Georgia Press, 1977).

[20] Leon Edel and Gordon N. Ray, eds., Henry James and H.G. Wells (Urbana: University of Illinois Press, 1958), p. 17.

[21] Ibid., 18ff.

[22] Edel, ed., The Selected Letters of Henry James, pp. 157-58.

[23] Elsa Nettels (James and Conrad) has much to say about James and Conrad and the question of mutual influence. Although pointing out the difficulties of ascertaining the degree of specific influence, she suggests that there were many similarities between the two authors, e.g., their employment of different perspectives on their subject, gradual disclosure of facts, definition of the novel as a picture and of characters as portraits, use of irony and of themes of guilt and betrayal, placing characters in a situation, sense of the fulfilling nature of the writer's life, etc.

[24] John Berryman, Stephen Crane, p. 237.

[25] Eric Solomon, Stephen Crane in England (Columbis, Ohio: Ohio State University Press, 1964), p. 82.

[26] In a letter to H.G. Wells of June 17, 1900, quoted in Edel and Ray, eds., op. cit., 67.

[27]See Edel and Ray, eds., op. cit., pp. 153-54.

[28]See Arthur Mizener, The Saddest Story (New York and Cleveland: The World Publishing Company, 1971), p. 50.

[29]Ford, Return to Yesterday, p. 205.

[30]Ford, Thus to Revisit (New York: Octagon Books, 1966 [first published in 1921]), pp. 46-47.

[31]For example, The Benefactor and An English Girl.

[32]Killigrew, ed., op. cit., 135.

[33]Joseph Conrad, A Sketch, p. 34.

[34]Jessie Conrad, Joseph Conrad as I Knew Him (London: Wm. Heinemann Ltd., 1926), p. ix.

[35]Jocelyn Baines, Joseph Conrad (London: Weidenfeld and Nicolson, 1960), p. 235.

[36]See Jessie Conrad, Joseph Conrad and His Circle, p. 75.

[37]See Borys Conrad, My Father: Joseph Conrad (London: Calder & Boyars, 1970), 25ff.

[38]Jessie Conrad, Joseph Conrad and His Circle, p. 75.

[39]C. Lewis Hind, Authors and I (New York, London: John Lane, 1921), p. 61.

[40]Jessie Conrad, Joseph Conrad and His Circle, p. 56.

[41]Baines, op. cit., 204.

[42]Edward Garnett, ed., Letters from Joseph Conrad, 1895-1924 (Indianapolis: Bobbs-Merrill Co., 1928), pp. 11-12.

40

[43] Quoted in Carl Bohnenberger and Norman M. Hill, eds., "The Letters of Joseph Conrad to Stephen and Cora Crane," Bookman, 69 (May, 1929; June, 1929), 372.

[44] Jessie Conrad, Joseph Conrad and His Circle, p. 131.

[45] Letter of October 20, 1905, included in the H.G. Wells Collection, University of Illinois Library.

[46] The other letters here cited are to be found in the H.G. Wells Collection in the University of Illinois Library.

[47] Quoted in Hart-Davis, op. cit., p. 168.

[48] Letter of November 1, 1906, included in Letters to Conrad, edited with an introduction by G. Jean-Aubry, First Editions Club (London: Curwen Press, 1926), no page. Even allowing for James's habitual use of what Leon Edel called "cushion words," the "mere twaddle of graciousness" (Edel, ed., The Selected Letters of Henry James, p. xxv), this compliment strikes one as genuine.

[49] Letter of December 5, 1897 to Edward Garnett, included in G. Jean-Aubry, Joseph Conrad, Life and Letters (Garden City, N.Y.: Doubleday, Page & Co., 1927), p. 211.

[50] Baines, op. cit., 205.

[51] Ibid.

[52] Letter of November 11, 1897, included in Letters to Conrad, no pagination.

[53] See Bohnenberger and Hill, op. cit., p. 232.

[54] See Grover Smith, Ford Madox Ford (New York and London: Columbia University Press, 1972), p. 11.

[55] Ford Madox Ford, Joseph Conrad (A Personal Remembrance) (Boston: Little, Brown, 1924), p. 45.

[56] Ibid., p. 48.

[57] Hugh Kenner, Gnomon (New York: McDowell, Obolensky, 1958), pp. 169-70.

[58] Ford, Joseph Conrad, p. 30.

[59] Ibid., p. 183.

[60] Ibid., p. 222.

[61] Ibid., p. 26.

[62] Ibid., p. 267.

[63] Harris Wilson, ed., Arnold Bennett and H.G. Wells (London: Rupert Hart-Davis, 1960), p. 16.

[64] H.G. Wells, Experiment in Autobiography (New York: The MacMillan Co., 1934), p. 522.

[65] Ibid., p. 524.

[66] Ibid., p. 525.

[67] Ibid., p. 526.

[68] Ibid., p. 527.

[69] Ibid., p. 526.

[70] W. Warren Wagar, ed., H.G. Wells (London: The Bodley Head, 1964), p. 203.

[71] Letter of April 9, 1913 from Wells to James, included in the H.G. Wells Collection.
Or, one might cite an earlier letter from Wells to Arnold Bennett, about The Wings of the Dove, "a book to read in and learn from" (included in Wilson, ed., op. cit., p. 84).

[72] Lovat Dickson, H.G. Wells: His Turbulent Life and Times (New York: Atheneum, 1969), p. 105.

[73] Letter of November 19, 1934, from Jessie Conrad to H.G. Wells, in the Wells Collection.

[74] The Book of Catherine Wells (with an introduction by her husband, H.G. Wells) (London: Chatto and Windus, 1928), p. 18. Among the other participants, Wells notes, were Arnold Bennett, Noel Coward, Roger Fry, Frank Swinnerton and Charlie Chaplin.

[75] Dickson, op. cit., p. 81.

[76] Ibid., p. ix.

[77] Wells, Experiment in Autobiography, p. 531.

[78] See Gordon N. Ray, "H.G. Wells Tries to Be a Novelist," included in Edwardians and Late Victorians, edited by Richard Ellmann (New York: Columbia University Press, 1960).

[79] One notes James's comment, "You must at moments make dear old Dickens turn--for envy of the eye and the ear and the nose and the mouth of you--in his grave" (letter of October 4, 1909, included in the Wells Collection).

[80] Wells remained perpetually suspicious, for example, of Conrad's "adorned" prose. If depicting a scene involving a boat lying in the water, he would, he declared, unlike Conrad, "in nineteen cases out of twenty . . . just let the boat be there in the commonest phrases possible" (quoted in Patrick Parrinder, H.G. Wells [Edinburgh: Oliver and Boyd, 1970], p. 14).

[81] Letters of September 23, 1913 and April 25, 1911, from Wells to James, included in the Wells Collection.

[82] See Parrinder, op. cit., p. 90.

[83]Wells, Experiment in Autobiography, p. 432.

[84]Letter of July 8, 1915, in the Wells Collection.

[85]Letter of July 10, 1915, in the Wells Collection.

[86]Letters of March 3, 1911 and July 6, 1915, in the Wells Collection.

[87]Vincent Brome, H.G. Wells (London, New York, Toronto: Longmans, Green & Co., 1951), p. 230.

[88]Letter of October 18, 1912, from James to Wells, in the Wells Collection.

[89]Dickson, op. cit., p. 212.

[90]John A. Meixner, Ford Madox Ford's Novels (Minneapolis, Minnesota: University of Minnesota Press, 1962), p. 272.

[91]Ibid., p. 273.

[92]Cited in ibid., p. 4.

[93]Ford, Thus to Revisit, p. 57.

[94]Paul L. Wiley, Ford Madox Ford: Novelist of Three Worlds (Syracuse, N.Y.: Syracuse University Press, 1962), p. 39.

[95]Carol Ohmann, Ford Madox Ford (Middletown, Connecticut: Wesleyan University Press, 1964), p. 4.

[96]Ford Madox Ford, Mightier than the Sword (London: George Allen & Unwin, Ltd., 1938), p. 54. Ford, after quoting Crane's remark, comments, "That is almost like having the Victoria Cross."

[97]See Violet Hunt, I Have This to Say (New York: Boni and Liveright, 1926), p. 44.

[98]One such reference occurs in Ford's Mightier than the Sword. Speaking of the company at Brede Place, he declares that there was always on hand "at least one just soul who was really devoted to Steevie--Conrad, or occasionally the Old Man [James] himself, or Mr. Garnett, or Harold Frederic, or Robert Barr, all strong and good men in their day" (Mightier than the Sword, p. 49).

[99]Ford, Thus to Revisit, p. 107.

[100]Ford, Mightier than the Sword, p. 41.

[101]Ibid.

[102]Ford, Thus to Revisit, p. 111.

[103]Ford, Return to Yesterday, p. 37.

[104]See page 8.

[105]Killigrew, ed., op. cit., p. 136.

[106]See Mizener, op. cit., p. 241.

[107]If not lovable, still, James could be benevolent, Ford pointed out, as in his concern for Crane in his last days.

[108]Ford, Mightier than the Sword, p. 145.

[109]Letter of November 20, 1908 from Ford to Wells, included in the Wells Collection.

[110]Ford Madox Ford, Portraits from Life (Boston, New York: Houghton Mifflin Co., 1937), pp. 120-121.

[111]Ibid., p. 115.

[112]"The eternally benevolent adviser of humanity," Ford called him in 1937 (ibid., p. 348), whereas Wells said, in 1945, that Ford was "crazy" after World War I (cited in Douglas Goldring, Trained for Genius [New York: E.P. Dutton & Co., 1949], p. 90).

[113] Ford, Return to Yesterday, p. 21.

[114] Frank MacShane, The Life and Work of Ford Madox Ford (New York: Horizon Press, 1965), p. 41.

[115] See Killigrew, ed., op. cit., p. 228.

[116] Ibid., p. 212.

[117] Goldring, op. cit., p. 128.

[118] Killigrew, ed., p. 212.

[119] Ford himself said, in 1921, that he fancied neither novel had "any great artistic value" (Thus to Revisit, p. 35).

[120] See Mizener, op. cit., p. 57.

[121] Ibid., p. 73.

[122] See Charles G. Hoffman, Ford Madox Ford (New York: Twayne Pub. Inc., 1967), p. 27.

[123] Killigrew, ed., op. cit., p. 218.

[124] Quoted in MacShane, op. cit., p. 42. Ford himself spoke of the "infinite mental patience" involved in the process of digging out words in the same room with Conrad (see ibid., p. 228).

[125] See R.W. Lid, Ford Madox Ford (Berkeley, California: University of California Press, 1964), p. 12.

[126] Clearly, Ford thought so, too, as the many references, among his reminiscences, to those enthusiastically endless debates (which could always rouse Conrad from his "fits of Slav-Oriental despair") unmistakably suggest. (See Ford, The March to Literature [London: George Allen & Unwin, Ltd., 1938], p. 763.)

[127] Letter (undated, but assumed to be written in 1903), from Ford to Wells, included in the Wells Collection.

[128] Ford Madox Ford, Ancient Lights (London: Chapman and Hall, Ltd., 1911), p. 293.

[129] R.W. Lid uses this term in speaking of Ford's viewing the "community" as a tangible one, "in which one man helped another" (Lid, op. cit., p. 25).

[130] Solomon, Stephen Crane in England, p. 10.

[131] Ibid., p. 11.

[132] Ibid., p. 12.

[133] Ibid., p. 13.

[134] Ibid., p. 31.

[135] See Larzer Ziff, The American 1890s (New York: The Viking Press, 1966), p. 201.

[136] Quoted in Berryman, Stephen Crane, p. 186.

[137] See Lillian Gilkes, Cora Crane (Bloomington, Indiana: Indiana University Press, 1960), p. 134.

[138] Quoted in Vincent Starrett, Buried Caesars (Chicago: Covici, McGhee Co., 1923), p. 85.

[139] Crane wrote an obituary of Frederic, appearing in the Chicago Chap-Book of March 15, 1898.

[140] Solomon, Stephen Crane in England, p. 68.

[141] See note 26.

[142] See Beer, Stephen Crane, p. 166.

[143] See Solomon, op. cit., p. 86.

[144] Quoted in Berryman, op. cit., p. 237.

[145] Beer, op. cit., p. 170.

[146] Berryman, op. cit., pp. 237-8.

[147] Solomon, op. cit., p. 65.

[148] Ford, Mightier Than the Sword, p. 57.

[149] H.G. Wells, "Stephen Crane. From an English Standpoint," North American Review, 171 (August, 1900), 241-42.

[150] See Gordon Ray, "H.G. Wells Tries to Be a Novelist," op cit., p. 111.

[151] This view was promulgated primarily by Edward Garnett, who declared that Crane "simply never knew how good his best work was" (Edward Garnett, Friday Nights [New York: Alfred A. Knopf, 1922], p. 203). In fairness to Garnett, it must be added that he saw Crane as writing against time and to cope with mounting debts and thus writing too much and at times carelessly. Garnett praised him, then and later, as a unique genius.

[152] Solomon, op. cit., pp. 46-47.

[153] Wells, Experiment in Autobiography, p. 522.

[154] Letter from H.G. Wells to Cora Crane of June 13, 1900, included in the Wells Collection.

[155] Solomon, op. cit., p. 89.

[156] Letter from Conrad to Crane of November 16, 1897, quoted in R.W. Stallman and Lillian Gilkes, Stephen Crane: Letters (New York: New York University Press, 1960), p. 151.

[157] Letter of January 13, 1899. See ibid., p. 205.

[158] Joseph Conrad, "Stephen Crane. A Note Without Dates," Bookman, 50 (February, 1920), 531.

[159] Beer, op. cit., p. 7.

[160]Samuel Hynes, Edwardian Occasions (New York: Oxford University Press, 1972), p. 48. Elsa Nettels's view does not quite coincide. Though citing James's statement that "the best things come, as a general thing, from talents that are members of a group; every man works better when he has companions working in the same line, and yielding the stimulus of suggestion, comparison, emulation," she indicates that James still disliked labels and proscribed doctrine, as did Conrad, and declares that, even if James, Conrad, Crane and Ford were no doubt united by their dedication to the art of fiction, their concern with form and style, their study of Flaubert and Maupassant, ". . . the impulse to transform the writers in England into a cohesive group came only from Ford" (Nettels, op. cit., p. 7).

[161]See Stallman and Gilkes, Stephen Crane: Letters, p. 344.

[162]See also Mrs. Joseph Conrad, "Recollections of Stephen Crane," Bookman, 63 (April, 1926), 134-137.

[163]Stanley Weintraub, in his book The London Yankees, sounds an echoing note: "Possibly no time and no place had ever experienced such an intense cultural cross-fertilization of expatriates from a single nation as had London--and England--by the Americans between 1894 and 1914. The face of art and literature had been profoundly altered in both countries by the convergence" (Weintraub, op. cit., p. 379).
In his very interesting book dealing with American writers and artists who, in the 150 years after the opening of the nineteenth century, transplanted themselves to England, Weintraub endeavors to answer many questions about the expatriates' assimilation and accommodation. The complexities of the issue notwithstanding, he is able to conclude on a positive note: "There would have been poetry and fiction and painting without the London Yankees. Yet given the conjunctions and the interplay of personalities and loyalties, it is

difficult to believe that Anglo-American culture would have been the same" (ibid., p. 380).

BIBLIOGRAPHY

Manuscript Collections

Stephen Crane Papers, Clifton Waller Barrett
Library, University of Virginia
Harold Frederic Papers, Manuscript Division,
Library of Congress
H.G. Wells Papers, Rare Book Room, University of
Illinois Library

Articles

Atherton, Gertrude. "The American Novel in
England." Bookman, 30 (1910), 633-640.
Blackall, Jean F. "Frederic's Gloria Mundi as a
Novel of Education." The Markham Review, 3
(May, 1972), 41-46.
Bohnenberger, Carl and Norman M. Hill, eds. "The
Letters of Joseph Conrad to Stephen and Cora
Crane." Bookman, 69 (May, 1929, 367-374);
69 (June, 1929, 528-535).
Conrad, Joseph. "Stephen Crane. A Note Without
Dates." Bookman, 50 (February, 1920), 529-
531.
Conrad, Mrs. Joseph. "Recollections of Stephen
Crane." Bookman, 63 (April, 1926), 134-137.
Crane, Stephen. "Harold Frederic." The Chicago
Chap-book, VIII, 1898.
Fox, Austin M. "Stephen Crane and Joseph Conrad."
The Serif, 6 (December, 1969), 16-20.
Gilkes, Lillian B. "Stephen Crane and the Harold
Frederics." The Serif, 6 (December, 1969),
21-48.
Gordon, John D. "The Ghost at Brede Place."
Bulletin of the New York Public Library, 56
(December, 1952), 591-595.
Karl, Frederick R. "Conrad, Wells, and the Two
Voices." PMLA, 88 (October, 1973), 1049-
1065.

Owen, Guy, Jr. "Crane's 'The Open Boat' and
    Conrad's 'Youth.'" Modern Language Notes, 73
    (February, 1958), 100-102.
Wells, H.G. "Stephen Crane. From an English
    Standpoint." North American Review, 171
    (August, 1900), 233-242.

Books

Baines, Jocelyn. Joseph Conrad. London:
    Weidenfeld and Nicolson, 1960.
Beer, Thomas. Stephen Crane. Garden City, N.Y.:
    Garden City Publishing Company, Inc., 1927.
Belgion, Montgomery. H.G. Wells. London, New
    York, Toronto: Longmans, Green & Co., 1953.
Berryman, John. Stephen Crane. New York: William
    Sloane Associates, 1950.
The Book of Catherine Wells. London: Chatto and
    Windus, 1928.
Borrello, Alfred. H.G. Wells. Carbondale,
    Illinois: Southern Illinois University Press,
    1972.
Briggs, Austin, Jr. The Novels of Harold Frederic.
    Ithaca and London: Cornell University Press,
    1969.
Brome, Vincent. H.G. Wells. London, New York,
    Toronto: Longmans, Green & Co., 1951.
Cassell, Richard M. Ford Madox Ford. Baltimore,
    Maryland: Johns Hopkins University Press,
    1961.
Conrad, Borys. My Father, Joseph Conrad. London:
    Calder & Boyars, 1970.
Conrad, Jessie. Joseph Conrad As I Knew Him.
    London: Wm. Heinemann Ltd., 1926.
Conrad, Jessie. Joseph Conrad and His Circle.
    New York: E.P. Dutton & Co., Inc., 1935.
Costa, Richard H. H.G. Wells. New York: Twayne
    Publishers, Inc., 1967.
Dickson, Lovat. H.G. Wells: His Turbulent Life
    and Times. New York: Atheneum, 1969.
Earnest, Ernest. Expatriates and Patriots.
    Durham, N.C.: Duke University Press, 1968.
Edel, Leon and Gordon N. Ray, eds. Henry James
    and H.G. Wells. Urbana, Illinois: University
    of Illinois Press, 1958.

Edel, Leon, ed. The Selected Letters of Henry
James. New York: Farrar, Straus & Cudahy,
1955.
Ellmann, Richard, ed. Edwardians and Late Vic-
torians. New York: Columbia University Press,
1960.
Ford, Ford Madox. Ancient Lights. London:
Chapman and Hall, Ltd., 1911.
Ford, Ford Madox. Henry James, A Critical Study.
New York: Octagon Books, 1969 (first pub-
lished 1913).
Ford, Ford Madox. Joseph Conrad (A Personal Re-
membrance). Boston: Little, Brown, 1924.
Ford, Ford Madox. The March to Literature.
London: George Allen & Unwin, Ltd., 1938.
Ford, Ford Madox. Mightier Than the Sword.
London: George Allen & Unwin, Ltd., 1938.
Ford, Ford Madox. Portraits from Life. Boston,
New York: Houghton Mifflin Co., 1937.
Ford, Ford Madox. Return to Yesterday. New York:
Horace Liveright, Inc., 1932.
Ford, Ford Madox. Thus to Revisit. New York:
Octagon Books, 1966 (first published 1921).
Garner, Stanton. Harold Frederic. Minneapolis:
University of Minnesota Press, 1969.
Garnett, Edward. Friday Nights. New York: Alfred
A. Knopf, 1922.
Garnett, Edward, ed. Letters from Joseph Conrad,
1895-1924. Indianapolis: Bobbs-Merrill Co.,
1924.
Gilkes, Lillian. Cora Crane. Bloomington,
Indiana: Indiana University Press, 1960.
Goldring, Douglas. South Lodge. London: Constable
& Co., Ltd., 1943.
Goldring, Douglas. Trained for Genius. New York:
E.P. Dutton & Co., 1949.
Gullason, Thomas A., ed. Stephen Crane's Career.
New York: New York University Press, 1972.
Hart-Davis, Rupert. Hugh Walpole. New York:
MacMillan, 1952.
Hind, C. Lewis. Authors and I. New York, London:
Weidenfeld and Nicolson, 1960 (first pub-
lished 1921).
Hind, C. Lewis. More Authors and I. London: John
Lane, 1922.

Hoffmann, Charles G. Ford Madox Ford. New York:
Twayne Publishers, Inc., 1967.
Holton, Milne. Cylinder of Vision: the Fiction
and Journalistic Writing of Stephen Crane.
Baton Rouge, La.: Louisiana State University
Press, 1972.
Hunt, Violet. I Have This to Say. New York: Boni
and Liveright, 1926.
Hynes, Samuel. Edwardian Occasions. New York:
Oxford University Press, 1972.
Jean-Aubry, G. Joseph Conrad: Life and Letters.
Garden City, N.Y.: Doubleday, Page & Co.,
1927.
Jean-Aubry, G., ed. Letters to Conrad. London:
Curwen Press, 1926.
Joseph Conrad, A Sketch. Garden City, N.Y.:
Doubleday Page & Co., 1924.
Katz, Joseph, ed. Stephen Crane in Transition.
DeKalb, Illinois: Northern Illinois Univer-
sity Press, 1972.
Kenner, Hugh. Gnomon. New York: McDowell,
Obolensky, 1958.
Killigrew, Michael, ed. Your Mirror to My Times
(The Selected Autobiographies and Impressions
of Ford Madox Ford). New York: Holt,
Rinehart, Winston, 1971.
Leer, Norman. The Limited Hero in the Novels of
Ford Madox Ford. East Lansing, Michigan:
Michigan State University Press, 1966.
Lid, R.W. Ford Madox Ford. Berkeley, California:
University of California Press, 1964.
Ludwig, Richard M. Letters of Ford Madox Ford.
Princeton, N.J.: Princeton University Press,
1965.
McKenzie, Norman and Jeanne. H.G. Wells. New
York: Simon and Schuster, 1973.
MacShane, Frank. The Life and Work of Ford Madox
Ford. New York: Horizon Press, 1965.
Meixner, John A. Ford Madox Ford's Novels.
Minneapolis: University of Minnesota Press,
1962.
Mizener, Arthur. The Saddest Story (A Biography
of Ford Madox Ford). New York, Cleveland:
The World Publishing Co., 1971.

Nettels, Elsa. James and Conrad. Athens, Georgia:
    University of Georgia Press, 1977.
O'Donnell, Thomas F. and Hoyt C. Franchere.
    Harold Frederic. New York: Twayne Publishers,
    Inc., 1961.
Ohmann, Carol. Ford Madox Ford. Middletown,
    Connecticut: Wesleyan University Press, 1964.
Parrinder, Patrick. H.G. Wells. Edinburgh:
    Oliver & Boyd, 1970.
Raknem, Ingvald. H.G. Wells and His Critics.
    Oslo: Universitetsforlaget, 1962.
Smith, Grover. Ford Madox Ford. New York and
    London: Columbia University Press, 1972.
Solomon, Eric. Stephen Crane in England.
    Columbus, Ohio: Ohio State University Press,
    1964.
Stallman, Robert and Lillian Gilkes. Stephen
    Crane: Letters. New York: New York
    University Press, 1960.
Stallman, Robert, ed. Stephen Crane: an Omnibus.
    New York: Alfred Knopf, 1952.
Starrett, Vincent. Buried Caesars. Chicago:
    Covici, McGhee Co., 1923.
Swinnerton, Frank. The Georgian Scene. New York:
    Farrar & Rinehart, 1934.
Wagar, W. Warren, ed. H.G. Wells. London: The
    Bodley Head, 1964.
Weintraub, Stanley. The London Yankees (Portraits
    of American Writers and Artists in England).
    New York & London: Harcourt Brace,
    Jovanovich, 1979.
Wells, H.G. Experiment in Autobiography. New
    York: Macmillan, 1934.
Wiley, Paul L. Ford Madox Ford: Novelist of Three
    Worlds. Syracuse, N.Y.: Syracuse University
    Press, 1962.
Wilson, Harris, ed. Arnold Bennett and H.G. Wells.
    London: Rupert Hart-Davis, 1960.
Ziff, Larzer. The American 1890s. New York: The
    Viking Press, 1966.

Index

About the Author

Gordon Milne was born in Haverhill, Massachusetts, and educated at Brown and Harvard Universities. He served in the United States Naval Reserve as a communications officer in 1942-1946 and holds the rank of LCDR, USNR, Retired. He is a professor of English at Lake Forest College, former Chairman of the Department of English, and currently Chairman of the American Studies Program. He was a Fulbright Guest Professor at Würzburg University in Germany in 1958-1959. He is the author of George William Curtis and the Genteel Tradition (1956), The American Political Novel (1966), and The Sense of Society: A History of the American Novel of Manners (1977).